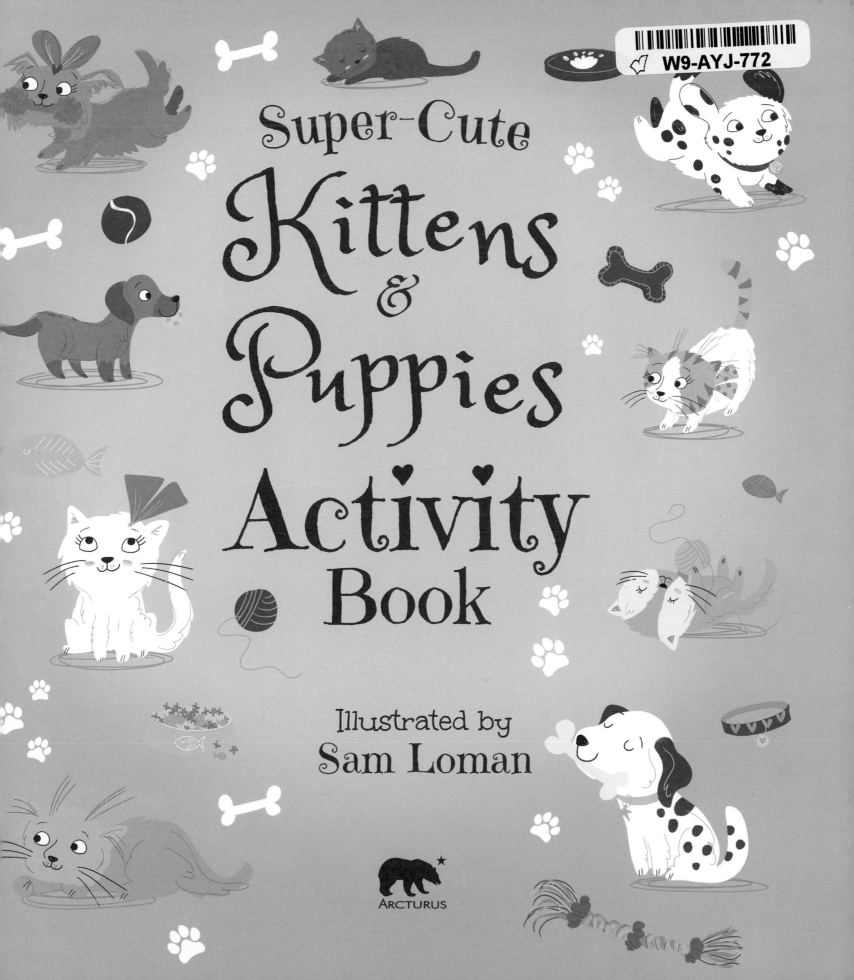

Super-Cute Kittens & Puppies Activity Book

Illustrated by
Sam Loman

ARCTURUS

ARCTURUS

This edition published in 2020 by Arcturus Publishing Limited
26/27 Bickels Yard, 151–153 Bermondsey Street,
London SE1 3HA

Illustrated by Sam Loman
Written by Sam Williams
Edited by Donna Gregory
Designed by squareandcircus.co.uk

ISBN: 978-1-83857-607-3
CH007380NT
Supplier 29 Date 0220 Print run 8513

Printed in China

Come On In!

Do you love puppies and kittens? Then come and meet these cuties. They have the waggiest tails and the fluffiest fur, and they love to play all day long. But which pathway leads to the house? Is it A, B, or C?

A

B

C

Picnic Fun!

The furry pet friends are having a picnic. Can you complete the scene by filling in the missing pieces?

Draw Me!

Follow these simple steps to create your very own adorable puppy.

Which Way?

Find a way for Oscar the daschund to sniff his way through the meadow and get his toy. Can you help him find his way? He can go up, down, left, or right, but not diagonally. He has to step on the flowers in this set order:

Treat Time

Scout has made a list of all the things he wants at his party. Can you find all the words in the grid below? Words are spelled out forward, backward, and diagonally.

F	R	I	E	N	D	S	R	E	B	A	L
E	A	S	I	T	E	E	F	A	U	N	N
T	B	N	E	G	E	S	R	B	R	O	B
R	A	S	L	L	E	S	I	F	E	N	R
E	B	O	N	E	L	O	S	L	A	N	O
A	E	R	S	R	O	B	B	U	T	A	T
T	D	N	E	A	G	U	E	R	S	B	H
S	S	S	S	I	S	T	E	R	E	Y	E
B	F	A	L	L	B	E	U	G	R	E	R
F	T	E	R	R	O	G	H	R	E	B	O
N	E	B	A	L	L	O	O	N	S	G	U
S	A	U	S	A	G	E	S	T	R	T	S

BONE   BALLOONS   BROTHER

FRISBEE   FRIENDS   SAUSAGES

BEDS   SISTER   TREATS

Birthday Surprises

It's Petra's birthday party. Can you figure out what each of her furry friends has brought her? Unscramble the letters to find out.

arlocl

airhbruhs

luddyc yot

lacekenc

zulpze okob

Copy Cat

Carefully copy this picture of Sadie using the grid below to help you.

Find the Kitten

The puppies and kittens are playing hide and seek in the garden, and now it's time for the kittens to hide. Can you spot all ten of them?

Puppy Buddies

The puppies are getting ready for a walk. Which puppy doesn't have a best friend in a matching outfit?

Naptime Maze

Can you help Bella find the path back to her warm, cozy bed?

Start

Finish

Playtime

It's playtime and the puppies are chasing each other all around the garden.
Can you find eight differences between these two fun scenes?

Puppy Tails

Use your best pens and pencils to draw some cute little puppies.
Add as many ribbons and bows as you like!

Fairground Fun

The puppies and kittens have gone to the fairground, and their furry friends are there too. Look at the picture for two minutes, then turn the page and answer the questions without turning back.

Fairground Fun

1. Which ride is behind the hot dog stand?

2. How many ducklings are there?

3. There is a white kitten in the red bumper car—true or false?

4. What animal is holding the hammer?

5. Can you see the Sun?

6. How many animals are holding hot dogs?

Prom Prep

Ivana loves dressing up! She's getting ready for her prom, but which of these silhouettes is an exact match for her?

Tangled Kites

It's a windy day, and the puppies are flying their kites, but their strings are all in a tangle. Can you follow the lines to see which kite belongs to each puppy?

Fruity Fun

The kittens and puppies are at the market buying tasty fruit. Can you solve the equations to see which bowl contains the most fruit?

$10 + 5$

$25 - 6$

$8 + 8$

3×6

Fun in the Sun

The kittens and puppies are playing with their furry friends. Can you figure out which one hasn't come out to play?

Percy

Millie

Tricia

Indi

Bailey

Jemima

Gertie

How Many Spots?

Spot has invited his brothers and sisters to play. Which of these cuties has the highest number of spots?

Pretty as a Picture

Violet can't decide which of her selfies she likes best. They are all identical except one. Can you figure out which one it is?

Heads or Tails?

Can you find a way from Scout the puppy's head to his tail? You can go up, down, left, or right, but not diagonally. Follow the footprints only in this order:

Start

Finish

Park Play

Bella is bringing lots of fun treats to the park. Can you find them all in the grid below? Words are spelled out forward, backward, and diagonally.

L	S	T	K	N	T	R	E	B	T	C	S
L	A	E	T	E	H	L	B	R	S	O	K
B	T	K	S	H	T	K	B	A	L	L	B
T	L	S	U	N	H	S	L	A	N	L	L
S	K	A	A	H	L	T	E	W	R	A	N
R	O	B	N	R	K	A	E	A	T	R	S
U	A	E	B	K	N	E	T	T	H	E	H
R	A	E	T	L	E	R	R	E	L	L	K
A	O	R	E	B	T	T	R	R	U	G	T
L	A	N	S	B	K	U	N	H	T	R	A
T	O	B	K	N	T	K	U	R	N	K	T
B	N	B	L	S	U	N	H	A	T	L	R

BONE   BLANKET   TREATS   SUNHAT

BALL   WATER   BASKET   COLLAR

Even Pets Love Pets!

It's the annual show, and the puppies and kittens have brought along their pets.
Can you see which pet belongs to who? Follow the tangled lines to find out.

Pretty Ribbons

Petra can't find her special bow. Can you help her? It's the only one that doesn't have an exact match, and she isn't already wearing it.

Ball Games

The puppies and kittens are playing with their bouncy balls, but Leia has lost hers. It's pink with gold stars. Can you help her find it?

Sparkling Snow

30

Snow has fallen overnight, and the furry friends are having fun. Can you spot these objects in this wintry scene?

2 red socks
3 green hats with red pompoms
3 pink mittens
4 green earmuffs

High Jumps!

These puppies have been awarded prizes for their jumping.
Work out what score each puppy got.

12 + 7

35 − 20

3 × 6

½ of 28

Follow the Smell

Bailey is so happy to smell the delicious sausages that his friend Daisy has grilled. Can you help him sniff his way through the maze to get there?

Start

Finish

Volleyball

The puppies and kittens are playing volleyball with their furry friends. Can you find these close-ups in the scene? Which one cannot be found?

Purr-Fect Portrait

Violet is painting a portrait of her best friend Ivana. Use your best pens and pencils to bring the portrait to life.

Follow the Trail

Look at the picture in the grid. Can you answer these questions?

1. In which square is the kitten that is in a basket?

2. Is there a collar in square E2?

3. Start at A1. Move two squares right and one square up. What do you see?

4. The cat in square E4 is wearing a pink ribbon: True or false?

5. In which square is the blue yarn?

Perfect Pet Name

The flower you think is the prettiest + the animal you think looks the sweetest = your ideal pet's name. For example, if you like the first flower and the first pet on the left, your pet's name would be Violet Petal.

Violet

Snow

Ruby

Pearl

Aqua

Rosa

Coral

Petal

Bubbles

Candy

Sunshine

Twinkle

Pickles

Pixie

Starry Toy

Solo is helping Bella find her special toy, which has two gold stars.
Can you help them to find it?

Pictures of Fun

Look at these photos with pictures of cute puppies in their winter outfits.
Can you tell which one doesn't have a matching pair?

40

Sleeping Pets

The kittens and puppies are having their afternoon naps.
Which one will sleep the longest?

1. The super-tired animal is a kitten.

2. She is in a basket.

3. She is already asleep.

All Snuggled Up

Decorate these lovely baskets so the tired pets can snuggle up and go to sleep. Goodnight!

Knittin' Kittens

The kittens have got their knitting into a tangle.
Can you see which item belongs to each kitten?

Poodle Doodle

Carefully copy this picture of Daisy.
Use the grid below to help you.

Toy Treasure!

The puppies have been busy collecting their toys together. Circle the collection with the highest number of points.

1	2	3	4	5

Queen Kitty

These cute kitties are playing at being princesses, and one will be crowned Queen for a day. Which one will it be? Solve the clues to see who it is.

1. She's wearing two pink ribbons.

2. Her tail is stripy.

3. Her eyes are open

Playtime Puzzle

Can you put the pieces of this cute scene back together again?
Which piece does not fit?

Precious Pet

Petra has lost her pet hamster, Nibbles.
Can you help her find him in this scene?

Hide-a-Kitty

It's time for lunch, but the kittens are hiding all around the house. Can you find all ten of them?

Finish the Picture

Can you draw the missing parts of these two cute kitties? Use your best pens and pencils, and let your imagination run wild.

Birthday Fun

It's Solo's birthday, and his family have hidden presents for him to find. Can you find all eleven of them?

Springtime Fun!

It's springtime and all the kittens and puppies have gone to the farm to meet the newborn lambs. Look at the picture for two minutes, then turn the page and answer the questions without looking back.

Springtime Fun!

1. How many butterflies are there?

2. Is the duckling's collar pink or blue?

3. Can you see a pond in the picture?

4. How many lambs are in the field?

5. Which animals are sitting on the fence?

Muddy Puppies

The puppies have been playing outdoors and are very muddy!
Which of these baths has the most rubber ducks?

Who is the Oldest?

All of these kittens go to the same daycare. But who is the oldest?
Solve the equations on their gifts to work out how many weeks old they are.

½ of 18

21 - 10

2 × 8

6 + 9

Poodle School!

Penny the poodle LOVES numbers. Help her finish this sudoku—each of the numbers 1–6 should appear in each row, column, and box.

6	1			5	
		5		6	2
	5		4		3
5		2		4	
4	2		5		
	6			2	5

Farmyard Fun

Jasper wants to join his friend. He can
go up, down, left, or right, but not diagonally.
He has to follow the balls of yarn in this order:

Start

Finish

Dream Dinner

Petra is feeling hungry. Can you draw in a delicious fish for her to eat? Add in some toys for her to play with afterward.

Twin Teaser

The furry friends are playing in the meadow.
Can you find the two identical twin kittens?

A Little Bit of Magic

Bring this cute scene to life using your best pens and pencils.

Butterfly Hunt

Tiger is searching for a special blue butterfly with stars on its wings. Can you help him find it?

Shadow Friends

Which of these shadows is an exact match for Scout and his furry friend?

Home Time

Jasper's had a great day playing outside, but now he needs to go home to his basket. Can you help him find a way through the maze?

Finish

Start

Draw Me

Follow the steps to create this cute kitty.
Add ribbons and bows!

1

2

3

4

Party Prep

Violet is getting ready for her party, and all her friends have come to help.
Can you tell which friend hasn't arrived yet?

Balloon Mix Up

The puppies and kittens have been to the fair and have each won a balloon, but their strings are all in a tangle. Follow the strings to see which item belongs to each pet?

67

Playful Puppies

Look at the cute picture in the grid. Can you answer these questions?

1. Start at A1. Move two squares right and two squares up. What do you see?

2. In which square is the dog with a pink ribbon?

3. True or false: The dog in square B4 is wearing a red collar?

4. What is in square E4?

5. In how many squares are the collar and leash?

Farmyard Friends

The puppies and kittens are at the farm, watching the baby lambs frolicking in the meadow. Which one of these lambs is different from all the rest?

Animal Trail

Can you help Oscar find a way through the farmyard to reach his friend Bailey? He has to follow the animals in this set order—chick, duckling, rabbit. He can go up, down, left, or right but not diagonally.

Start

Finish

Beach Birthday

The puppies are having a beach party! Solve the clues to see whose birthday it is.

1. Her tail has a pink ribbon on it.

2. She doesn't have a pink collar.

3. She's playing with a blue ball.

4. She isn't wearing a bow in her hair.

5. Her paws are white.

Flower Fun

The puppies and kittens are playing at the farm. Look at this picture for two minutes, then turn the page and see if you can get all the questions right!

Flower Fun

1. Is the mane of the horse nearest the farmhouse black or white?

2. How many bees are in the picture?

3. Are all of the kittens outside?

4. How many kittens are there altogether?

5. What is the ginger kitten chasing—a butterfly or a ball?

It's Magic!

It's Halloween, and the puppies and kittens are dressing up. How many pumpkins can you spot?

Paint the Rainbow

A beautiful rainbow has appeared. Use your best pens and pencils to finish the picture.

On the Ice

Spot and his friends are having fun on the ice. Can you spot eight differences between these two chilly scenes?

Paint the Puppies

Use your best pens and pencils or paints to bring this super-cute scene of playful (and sleepy!) puppies to life.

Craft Fair

Leia has been making lots of cool, crafty items for the fair. Can you find all of these things in this cute scene?

3 pairs of knitted mittens

3 birthday cards

3 dreamcatchers

6 bags of fudge

Snowcat

Jemima has made four snowcats, but one has been made with a slight difference. Can you see which it is?

Dress Up

Look at this jigsaw of the kittens tidying up their bedroom.
Which piece fits into the puzzle?

You Choose

What would your perfect kitten look like, and what cute name would you choose? Use your imagination to finish this picture.

Where's Millie's Bone?

Millie has lost her bone. Can you help her find a way through the maze to reach it?

Start

Finish

Answers

page 3 Come On In!

page 4 Picnic Fun!

page 6 Which Way?

page 7 Treat Time

page 8 Birthday Surprises

collar hairbrush cuddly toy

necklace

puzzle book

page 10 Find the Kitten

page 11 Puppy Buddies

page 12 Naptime Maze

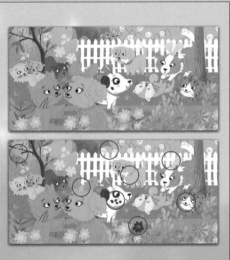

page 13 Playtime

1. Ferris wheel
2. 4
3. True
4. A stripy kitten
5. No
6. 2

page 18 Fairground Fun

page 19 Prom Prep

page 20 Tangled Kites

page 21 Fruity Fun

page 22 Fun in the Sun

page 23 How Many Spots?

page 24 Pretty as a Picture

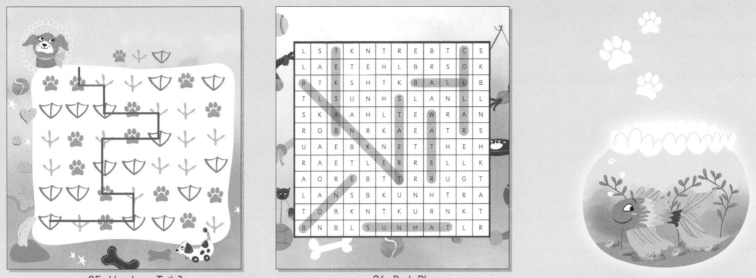

page 25 Heads or Tails?

page 26 Park Play

page 27 Even Pets Love Pets!

page 28 Pretty Ribbons

page 29 Ball Games

page 30–31 Sparkling Snow

12 + 7
19

3 × 6
18

35 – 20
15

½ of 28
14

page 32 High Jumps

page 33 Follow the Smell

page 34 Volleyball

1. A5

2. No

3. Bowl of cat food

4. True

5. C1

page 37 Follow the Trail

page 39 Starry Toy

page 40 Pictures of Fun

page 41 Sleeping Pets

page 43 Knittin' Kittens

page 45 Toy Treasure!

page 46 Queen Kitty

page 47 Playtime Puzzle

page 48 Precious Pet

page 49 Hide-a-Kitty

page 51 Birthday Fun

1. 4

2. Blue

3. No

4. 5

5. A rabbit, a duckling, and 3 chicks

page 54 Springtime Fun!

page 55 Muddy Puppies

page 56 Who is the Oldest?

page 57 Poodle School!

page 58 Farmyard Fun

page 60 Twin Teaser

page 62 Butterfly Hunt

page 63 Shadow Friends

page 64 Home Time

page 66 Party Prep

page 67 Balloon Mix Up

1. **Plate of doggy treats**

2. **D2**

3. **True**

4. **Ball**

5. **4**

page 69 Playful Puppies

page 70 Farmyard Friends

page 71 Animal Trail

page 72 Beach Birthday

1. White
2. 7
3. No
4. 10
5. Butterfly

page 74 Flower Fun

page 75 It's Magic!

page 77 On the Ice

page 79 Craft Fair

page 80 Snowcat

page 81 Dress Up

page 83 Where's Millie's Bone?